T0081068

YOU CHOOSE
BOOKS

APOLLO 11
MOON LANDING
An Interactive Space Exploration Adventure

by Thomas K. Adamson

Consultant:
Richard Bell, PhD
Associate Professor of History
University of Maryland, College Park

You Choose Books are published by Capstone Press,
1710 Roe Crest Drive, North Mankato, Minnesota 56003
www.mycapstone.com

Library of Congress Cataloging-in-Publication Data
Names: Adamson, Thomas K., 1970–
Title: Apollo 11 moon landing : an interactive space exploration adventure /
    by Thomas K. Adamson.
Description: North Mankato, Minnesota : Capstone Press, [2017] | Series: You
    choose books. You choose space | Audience: Age 8–12. | Audience: Grade 4
    to 6. | Includes bibliographical references and index.
Identifiers: LCCN 2016009132| ISBN 9781491481035 (library binding) | ISBN
    9781491481370 (pbk.) | ISBN 9781491481417 (ebook (pdf))
Subjects: LCSH: Project Apollo (U.S.)—History—Juvenile literature. | Space
    flight to the moon—History—20th century—Juvenile literature. |
    Moon—Exploration—20th century—Juvenile literature.
Classification: LCC TL789.8.U6 A472 2017 | DDC 629.45/4—dc23
LC record available at http://lccn.loc.gov/2016009132

Editorial Credits
Adrian Vigliano, editor; Kayla Rossow, designer;
Wanda Winch, media researcher; Laura Manthe, production specialist

Photo Credits
AP Images, 89; Getty Images: UIG/Sovfoto, 6; NASA, 12, 17, 36, 50, 105, Dryden
Flight Research Center, 28, 40, ESA/Hubble Heritage Team (STScI/AURA), nebula
design element, Johnson Space Center, cover, 23, 30, 44, 62, 67, 69, 82, 99, 100, 103,
Marshall Space Flight Center, 10; National Naval Aviation Museum Library: Robert
Lawson Photograph Collection, 72; Naval History & Heritage Command: photo by
Milt Putnam, HS-4, 92 [UA 44.02.01]; Newscom: CNP/NASA, 77; Shutterstock:
HelenField, lunar surface design, HorenkO, paper design

Printed in China.
5876

Table of Contents

ABOUT YOUR
ADVENTURE

YOU are living in the mid-1900s, a time of amazing breakthroughs in space exploration. People around the world watch as the United States tries to land astronauts on the moon.

In this book you'll explore how the choices people made meant the difference between life and death. The events you'll experience happened to real people.

Chapter One sets the scene. Then you choose which path to read. Follow the directions at the bottom of each page. The choices you make will change your outcome. After you finish your path, go back and read the others for new perspectives and more adventures.

YOU CHOOSE the path
you take through history.

6

Yuri Gagarin (front)

AN IMPOSSIBLE DREAM

You are an American in the 1960s. The United States and the Soviet Union have been in a space race since the end of World War II. In 1957 the Soviet Union launched a satellite called Sputnik. Since then, the two superpowers have increased their efforts to prove they have the best technology by attempting more and more daring feats in space.

In April 1961, the Soviet Union sends Yuri Gagarin into orbit around Earth in the tiny *Vostok* spacecraft. Gagarin becomes the first person in space. After one complete orbit around Earth, he lands safely.

Turn the page.

Less than a month later, on May 5, 1961, millions of people watch on live TV as Alan Shepard becomes the first American in space. The *Freedom 7* space capsule carried Shepard to an altitude of 116 miles (187 kilometers) for a 15-minute flight.

Afraid that the Soviets could gain superiority in the area of space technology, the U.S. government begins a program to develop more powerful rockets. When President John F. Kennedy addresses Congress on May 25, 1961, he sets an ambitious goal. "I believe that this nation should commit itself to achieving the goal, before this decade is out, of landing a man on the moon and returning him safely to the Earth." The finish line in the space race has been set.

With great urgency, the United States sets to work to learn how to get to space, live in space, and travel farther than anyone ever has. But Kennedy was right when he said, "no single space project in this period will be more impressive to mankind … and none will be so difficult or expensive to accomplish."

The new space program first begins flying more missions in Earth orbit. These Mercury missions are the country's first flights into space. They test technology to get astronauts into Earth orbit and return safely to Earth. Then the Gemini missions test the skills needed to go the moon. These missions have astronauts spend more time in space. They work on space walks and practice docking spacecraft together in space.

Turn the page.

10

Engineers and technicians put rockets
such as the Saturn V through hundreds
of hours of rough testing.

Finally, in 1966, Project Apollo begins. The first Apollo flights are unmanned tests of the huge Saturn V rocket, the only rocket powerful enough to send astronauts to the moon. These flights also test the lunar lander, the only spacecraft designed to fly in space and land on the moon.

You are excited to be involved with something as big and historic as a moon landing. It's an exciting age of space discovery and exploration, and you want to be a part of it.

To work on training for the Apollo 11 mission, turn to page 13.
To be in Mission Control for the Apollo 11 moon landing, turn to page 45.
To be on the astronaut recovery team, turn to page 73.

Pilots and engineers used early simulators
to train for how spacecraft would handle
at various speeds and altitudes.

CHAPTER 2

TRAINING FOR A DREAM MISSION

The moon launch is going smoothly so far. You watch your computer console from Mission Control at the Manned Spaceflight Center in Houston, Texas. The data tell you that the rocket's engine is performing normally. The flight controllers also carefully watch the data.

As the rocket's next stage ignites, one of the controllers says, "We have a leak in the CSM propulsion system." Fuel is slowly leaking out of the Command and Service Module (CSM), which would be the last stage to fire to send the astronauts to the moon. The team monitors the rate of the leak, but the launch continues.

13

Turn the page.

Suddenly, the engine shuts down. The Flight Dynamics Officer (FIDO), a flight controller who monitors the flight path, has two choices. He can instruct the astronauts to ignite the CSM engine to put them into orbit around Earth. They could then plan re-entry. Or, he could use the CSM engine to have the spacecraft splash down right away in the Atlantic Ocean. But because of the fuel leak, they aren't sure whether the engine has enough fuel.

You watch the FIDO try to decide which option to take. The spacecraft is moving at such a high speed that it travels 5 miles (8 km) for every second he delays. The flight director, who leads the flight controllers, steps in and orders an immediate abort to land in the Atlantic Ocean. The decision is too late. The crew lands in Africa's Atlas Mountains. The capsule's parachutes fail to open, and the crew is killed.

Good thing this isn't a real mission. It was a computer simulation. The flight controllers and astronauts performed several of these simulations to practice for the real moon missions. In this simulation, the crew would have died because of a delay in making a decision. The team learns from this mistake and works harder to make sure something like this would never happen in the real mission.

A manned mission to the moon will be the most complicated engineering task in history. It all has to go perfectly. It will take a lot of training.

To be on the team that works on simulations, turn to page 16.
To work in the Astronaut Office as the astronaut supervisor, turn to page 25.

You work on the team that plans what the astronauts and flight controllers will do during simulations. It feels a little weird to think of it this way, but your job is to try to make the team fail.

You throw problems at the team and try to kill the crew! Of course, this is to give them the chance to face these dangers in the safety of a simulated spacecraft sitting on the ground, controlled by computers.

The simulations are very realistic. Everyone takes them seriously. They treat them as though they were real flights. The team feels real tension during emergencies. This is the only way to know what the real mission would actually be like.

You have been working for several weeks on simulations, and the flight controllers and astronauts are learning what to do in all kinds of emergencies. They have had some successful missions in the simulators. The simulation supervisor (SimSup), who leads your team, decides it's time to challenge the trainees more.

NASA converted the cockpits of military aircraft for use as early flight simulators.

To work on a simulation that involves an engine failure, turn to page 18.
To work on a simulation that involves a computer malfunction, turn to page 20.

The SimSup says, "Let's give the astronauts an unrelated problem during the landing to see if they're paying attention." You have just the problem already in mind.

You've written a set of computer commands. Your program will tell the astronauts and flight controllers that there is a failure in the ascent stage engine. The ascent stage engine will launch the astronauts off the moon. It's not being used now, but it has to be monitored the whole time to make sure it will work when it needs to. While the team lands on the moon, you want to be sure they are also aware of getting off the moon.

The simulation team is keeping the flight controllers busy. They have to fix minor problems as they listen to the astronauts go through the landing procedure. You sneak in the program that tells them the ascent engine is not working.

One of the flight controllers notices and says, "Ascent stage not responding." The flight director responds immediately, "That's an abort. Tell the crew to abort the landing, CAPCOM." CAPCOM, or the capsule communicator, is the only flight controller who communicates directly with the astronauts.

You say to the flight director, "Good one, Flight. You nailed it."

You knew this was the correct and only decision that could have been made in this situation. Maybe you're not challenging the team enough, though. They could be ready for more.

Turn to page 22.

You and the team set up the computers for the simulation. You have written a set of computer commands that will distract the astronauts, Neil Armstrong, Edwin "Buzz" Aldrin, and Michael Collins, with a minor electrical problem on the spacecraft while attempting the landing. While they work on that, the program will tell the controllers that the Lunar Module (LM) main computer has failed.

You listen to the flight controllers go through the landing procedure. You then start your computer failure program. The FIDO sees the problem right away. "LM computer failure," he says.

The flight director waits for a second. He then snaps, "What do you recommend?"

The flight controller says, "Stand by." You know he is asking one of the other engineers for more data to see if the computer can switch over to a backup system. Finally, he says, "Switching to the backup system so the LM can abort!"

The flight director responds, an edge to his voice. "Never mind that. We're too late for the abort. We just splattered the crew across the Sea of Tranquility. We need quicker decisions!"

This time, you have won the battle. But the flight director isn't giving up either. "We've learned from this," he tells you. "We dare you to get us again."

21

To do another simulation, turn to page 22.
To move on to astronaut crew assignments for the moon landing, turn to page 31.

This landing attempt is too important for the country and the world for you programmers to ease up on the flight team now. This time, one simple problem will provide the challenge.

The landing simulator will have one of the thrusters become stuck firing and not be able to shut off. This will cause crew commander Neil Armstrong and pilot Edwin "Buzz" Aldrin to lose control. There's nothing they can do about that in flight. They will have to abort the mission. This will test the communication between the crew on the moon and the controllers on Earth.

You listen to the team during the simulation. Armstrong sees the problem right away. "We're losing altitude," he says. Then the lander appears to tip from side to side. "Altitude control is gone—the horizon is tilting like crazy." You hear Aldrin mutter, "Neil—hit abort."

But Armstrong doesn't abort the landing right away. He seems to be waiting for Houston to tell him what to do. He will need to act quickly or the Lunar Module could crash. Finally, Houston gives the order, "Apollo 11, abort!"

But it is too late. By the time Armstrong hits the abort button, the simulation ends. If this had been the real landing, they would have slammed into the lunar surface, destroying the lander. The astronauts would not have survived.

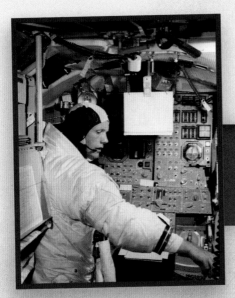

Neil Armstrong, working on a Lunar Module training session.

Turn the page.

Later, you talk to Armstrong. "What happened in there?"

He replies, "I wanted to see how quickly flight control would call for the abort."

"So you were testing them?" you ask.

"We don't need a successful landing in every simulation. I want to learn from these." With a smirk, Armstrong adds, "No one can die in a simulation."

You begin to feel confident of the crew's ability to land successfully because of your challenging simulations. By July 5, with the launch quickly approaching, the whole team seems to be ready for the real thing. The Apollo 11 primary crew has gone to Florida to prepare for the launch. There is time to do another simulation with the Apollo 12 backup crew.

To do no more simulations, turn to page 36.
To do one more simulation with the Apollo 12 backup crew, turn to page 37.

As head of the Astronaut Office in Houston, you supervise the astronauts, including their training and crew assignments. The astronauts will take survival training in case of an emergency landing in a remote location. They will fly on an airplane known as the "vomit comet." This KC-135A airplane flies in long up-and-steep-diving flights to simulate zero gravity. They will also learn a little bit about geology and fly a lunar lander simulator. They even learn how to pick up rocks while wearing space suits.

A lot of training has to get done, and you have to get going on something right away.

To work on lunar lander training, turn to page 26.
To work on geology training, turn to page 29.
To work on crew assignments, turn to page 31.

The astronauts train in a lunar lander simulator called the Lunar Landing Research Vehicle (LLRV). This awkward-looking aircraft has a jet engine pointing down during flight. The LLRV simulates the moon's gravity, which is one-sixth that of Earth. The LLRV gets as close as possible to simulating how the lander will fly on the moon. The pilot controls small thrusters to fly the craft.

On May 6, 1968, Director of Flight Operations Chris Kraft calls you. "Armstrong just had to bail on the LLRV." You know astronaut Neil Armstrong has already flown the LLRV several times during his training.

"What do you mean he had to bail?"

"He lost control. The thing tipped and swayed and then Neil ejected. The LLRV exploded a second later."

You're more worried about Armstrong than the machine. "Is Neil all right?"

"Yeah, he's fine. He parachuted safely to the ground. It was a close call, though."

You agree. "He's lucky to be alive. How did it happen?"

"One of the thrusters leaked propellant," Kraft says.

You start thinking that maybe those LLRVs are too risky. You're thinking about not allowing any more LLRV training.

To allow LLRV training to continue, turn to page 28.
To consider discontinuing LLRV training, turn to page 40.

Dangerous as the machine is, you agree that the LLRV training is needed for a successful landing. There's just no other way to simulate the landing. Nothing this important will get accomplished without some risk. You talk with the astronauts about it, and they all agree. Armstrong says flatly, "It's just good training."

With the question of LLRV training settled, you have another issue to work on. Which astronauts will be on the next Apollo crew?

NASA lost three LLRVs in training accidents between 1968 and 1971. All three pilots (including Armstrong) bailed out safely.

Turn to page 31.

Astronaut Neil Armstrong comes to you with a concern he has about the mission. "We're going to be working in place of geologists. We're only going to have about two hours to collect samples. It would be worthwhile if we knew a little bit about what we're doing."

You bring the idea of sending the astronauts for more geology training to Director of Flight Operations Chris Kraft. His response is not enthusiastic. "The goal is to get a man on the moon and return him to Earth safely. Not to do a lot of geology. There isn't time for that. We have to get the landing right or the Soviets might beat us there."

Turn the page.

He's right. For now, you just have to beat the Soviets to the moon. There will only be limited geology training.

You report back to Armstrong, "Just focus on getting yourself on the surface safely. Describe it with as much detail as you can when you're on the surface. The geologists will be listening."

With that, you turn your attention to who is going to fly which missions.

Neil Armstrong trains with a box designed to collect lunar rock samples.

Go to page 31.

You are in charge of assigning the crew members for each Apollo mission. As the teams prepare for the Apollo 9 and 10 test flights, it begins to look like Apollo 11 will be the first attempt at landing on the moon. It's time to assign the crew for that mission.

You start to realize what a huge decision this is. It's up to you to decide who makes history as the first man on the moon! His name will be remembered for centuries, maybe even longer.

It's clear that all of the astronauts are capable of making the landing. But are there some whose skills stand out as the best? Should it simply be whoever's turn is next to be assigned a moon mission?

To choose the team that has the best skills, turn to page 32.
To choose the team that is next in line, turn to page 42.

You know that the astronauts with the most experience in the lunar lander are Pete Conrad and Al Bean. You talk it over with astronaut Alan Shepard.

"Conrad is the backup for Apollo 8. So if we follow the way we have done it before, they train while the next two missions take place. Then they are assigned as the primary crew for the third mission."

Shepard says, "Apollo 11."

You say, "Right. Conrad and Bean have practically lived in those simulators. They'll do great."

However, before you can talk to Conrad and his crew about it, a NASA official calls you with a bold new plan. He tells you, "Apollo 8 is going to go to the moon."

You reply, "That's really pushing the schedule."

The NASA official replies, "We think the Soviets are planning something big. We just have to get there first, even if we don't land."

You know this means the crew rotation will have to change. Conrad and Bean are best at flying the Lunar Module, and Apollo 8 won't even bring the lander along. They will have to become the backup crew for Apollo 9, which will test-fly the lander and do the dockings. This change makes them the prime crew for Apollo 12.

Now Neil Armstrong and Buzz Aldrin will back up Apollo 8, which makes them the primary crew for Apollo 11. Since he is the commander of that crew, maybe you should make sure Armstrong is OK working with Aldrin, who would be flying the lander with him.

To get Armstrong's advice, turn to page 34.
To just go ahead with the crew assignment, turn to page 42.

While Apollo 8 is orbiting the moon in December 1968, you decide to talk to Armstrong. You tell him about assigning him and his crew of Aldrin and Collins to Apollo 11.

At this point, the plan is that Apollo 11 will be the first attempt at a landing, but that could still change. You know that Jim Lovell, in orbit around the moon right now, is an experienced pilot. You wonder whether you should ask Armstrong if the Lunar Module pilot should be Jim Lovell, or, instead, Buzz Aldrin, who has been working with Armstrong as the Apollo 8 backup crew.

To ask about Lovell, go to page 35.
To go ahead with Aldrin, turn to page 42.

You explain to Armstrong, "Lovell is reliable, and I wonder if you and he would work better together?"

Armstrong says, "Jim would be great to work with. We would certainly be able to count on him." Then he adds, "But everything seems to be going all right with Aldrin."

You tell Armstrong, "We just want the team that will give us the best chance at success."

Armstrong replies, "You're right. But it bothers me that Lovell would be pulled out of line. He deserves a shot at commanding his own mission. He would be in line to command Apollo 13 and land on the moon with that mission. Aldrin and I will work fine together."

You agree that this is the best option. "Ok, I'll call a meeting with you, Aldrin, and Michael Collins soon."

Turn to page 42.

You feel the crew and mission controllers are ready for the moon landing mission. The extra work might make the teams too exhausted for the mission. You have worked them hard enough, and now it's time for the real thing. You await the launch date hoping all goes as planned!

Apollo 11 astronauts Armstrong (left), Collins (center), and Aldrin.

THE END

To follow another path, turn to page 11.
To read the conclusion, turn to page 101.

The SimSup asks, "What do the flight controllers know about program alarms?"

You have to admit that program alarms have not been dealt with in simulations. "They're a minor problem and not likely to come up."

"Write a program for it," the SimSup replies.

You nod and get to work. If the flight controllers handle this right, the simulation should end in a successful landing.

In the landing simulation, everything is going perfectly. The computer then sends a message to the astronauts, which the guidance officer (GUIDO), who monitors navigational systems, also sees: "1201—Executive overflow—no vacant areas." This program alarm means the lander's computer is busy with calculations and cannot keep up.

Turn the page.

You hear GUIDO ask his software expert, "What's with this program alarm? Is anything wrong?" He has never seen this alarm before and there's nothing in his flight rules for it.

The software expert can't offer much help. "The computer is too busy to do everything it needs to do," he says.

It's up to GUIDO to make a recommendation based on this information, and quickly. You know this is the perfect test for the team's decisions. GUIDO sees nothing wrong with the computer—it's overloaded with information, but it's still working fine. It's the program alarm that concerns him.

GUIDO remembers the need to make quick decisions. He calls to the flight director, "Something is wrong in the computer … abort the landing!"

The flight director didn't see this coming. But he has to trust his team. He snaps at CAPCOM to tell the crew: "Abort, abort!"

You know the mistake the flight controllers made. You explain the program alarm to the flight director. While the computer was still doing its job, there was no problem. You give it to him straight, "This was not an abort. You should have continued the landing."

You schedule a few more hours of training on program alarms, including which ones don't require aborting the landing. GUIDO writes down the new mission rules: If the alarms are not continuous, the landing can continue. You have done your part to make the Apollo 11 moon landing a success!

THE END

To follow another path, turn to page 11.
To read the conclusion, turn to page 101.

You think the LLRVs are too risky. Continuing to fly them is just pressing your luck. But you want Armstrong's opinion before you send your negative report. You meet with him.

"Neil, tell me your honest opinion of the LLRVs."

His response surprises you, "Using them is absolutely essential."

The LLRV trained pilots to make the final stage of the Lunar Module descent. It simulated the feeling of landing in the moon's 1/6th gravity environment.

You respond, "But after what just happened to you, don't you think they're too dangerous?"

Armstrong simply says, "Yeah, they're dangerous, but they're the best training for landing on the moon."

How could the man who was just nearly killed in an LLRV accident still support using them? You ask the other astronauts and they all support it too. This is all you need to change your mind.

But you do agree with grounding the LLRVs until the problem can be studied. Engineers will need to work for several months on design improvements before astronauts fly the LLRVs again. Armstrong would fly the LLRV several more times about a month before the launch of Apollo 11.

THE END

To follow another path, turn to page 11.
To read the conclusion, turn to page 101.

You normally assign the backup flight crew for the current mission as the prime crew for the third mission after that. The backup crew for the Apollo 8 mission that orbited the moon was Armstrong, Aldrin, and Fred Haise. Command Module pilot Haise was substituting for Michael Collins, who had to have back surgery. Collins would soon return to duty on Armstrong and Aldrin's crew.

On January 4, 1969, it's time to get that crew confirmed for their mission. You call them into your office.

You get right to the point, "Because of Apollo 8's success, we will have two more test flights. If they go perfectly, we will attempt a landing with Apollo 11. And you've got the Apollo 11 flight."

The astronauts don't say anything at first. Maybe they are trying to hide their excitement at this news. You continue, "Apollo 9 and 10 will have to go perfectly. But we need to get everything set for a landing attempt."

The astronauts thank you. You can tell they are genuinely happy just to be a part of this mission. They remain professional because they know the first landing could just as easily be Apollo 12 or 13, or even 14. It just depends on how well the missions go. But Armstrong, Aldrin, and Collins are next in line, and you know they will train hard for this important mission.

43

THE END

To follow another path, turn to page 11.
To read the conclusion, turn to page 101.

The Apollo 11 crew launched successfully
on July 16, 1969, at 9:32 a.m.

CHAPTER 3

THE BIG DAY

The big day has arrived. Today, July 20, 1969, you hope to help fulfill President Kennedy's goal of landing a man on the moon before the end of the decade.

Astronauts Neil Armstrong and Edwin "Buzz" Aldrin have moved into the Lunar Module (LM), which is called *Eagle*. They are flying the spacecraft toward the moon's surface. Meanwhile, Mike Collins is in the Command Module (CM), called *Columbia*, in orbit around the moon. He will keep that part of the spacecraft ready for Armstrong and Aldrin's return from the surface. If the mission goes as planned, they will become the first humans ever to land and walk on a surface other than Earth.

Turn the page.

In simulations, the landing was always the big moment. Inside Mission Control of the Manned Spaceflight Center in Houston today, it feels just like a simulation. The only difference is all the people in the viewing room behind the glass watching.

You and the other flight controllers in Mission Control are watching your computer consoles intently. You monitor data about the spacecraft, the health of the astronauts, and the computers. If anything goes wrong, you or one of the other controllers will know it right away. Even though the tension is high, you have confidence in your abilities and in the astronauts flying 240,000 miles (386, 243 km) away.

Everyone in Mission Control has an important job. The flight engineers make sure the spacecraft is operating as it should. They solve the problems that come up. They are trained to make quick decisions to make sure the mission goes successfully. The capsule communicator, or CAPCOM, is another important job. This is the only flight controller who communicates directly with the astronauts.

To work in Mission Control as a flight engineer, turn to page 48.
To work in Mission Control as CAPCOM, turn to page 57.

You are the guidance officer, or GUIDO, for short. You're 26 years old, but that's not much younger than most of the other guys in the room. Your job is to keep track of the spacecraft's computers, landing radars, and navigation.

Gene Kranz, the flight director, is in charge of everyone in the room. Everyone calls him "Flight." You and the other flight controllers give him information and make suggestions. But he makes the final decisions. And what he says goes.

As the LM approaches the surface of the moon, Flight tells the flight controllers to listen. "Today is our day, and the hopes and dreams of the entire world are with us ... In the next hour we will do something that has never been done before ... The risks are high ... that is the nature of our work. You are a great team. One that I feel privileged to lead."

Inspired and ready to focus, you turn your attention to the LM computer readouts. The data coming from *Eagle* has been spotty. Sometimes it flows to your computer just fine, but sometimes communications stop.

You have enough data to notice that the LM is going to miss the planned landing site. The landing site is an oval 10 miles (16 km) long by 3 miles (4.8 km) wide. This area was chosen because it's flat, wide, and has few craters. But if they miss it, they could be in a more dangerous region.

You hear Armstrong say, "We went by the three-minute point early. We're going to land long." The astronauts use landmarks on the moon to track their progress. They missed this point by only 3 seconds. But that means about 3 miles (4.8 km) of distance.

Turn the page.

You need to give Flight a recommendation. You could let them keep going until you get better data. But this situation may be dangerous enough to require aborting the landing.

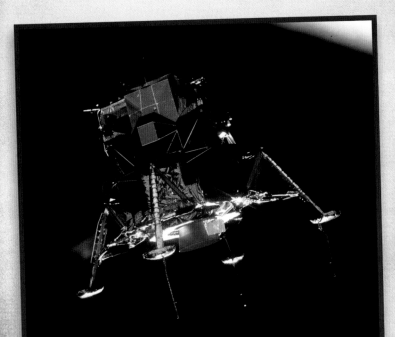

Because the Lunar Module was designed to fly only in space, there was no need to streamline it like an airplane or a rocket.

To tell Flight to continue, go to page 51.
To consider telling Flight to abort, turn to page 52.

You don't think the difference that Armstrong is reporting is great enough to call for an abort yet. It's close, though, so you warn Flight, "They're a little bit long. I'll watch it, and if it doesn't get worse, I think we'll make it."

Just then, you get fresh data from the LM. The data still say the LM is long, but it's not getting any worse. In fact, it's just barely within the mission rules for an abort. You give Flight a thumbs-up. CAPCOM says, "*Eagle*, you are go to continue powered descent."

51

Turn to page 54.

Missing the landing zone could be disastrous for the astronauts. They could end up landing in a rough area with boulders too big to avoid. They could end up in a crater on uneven ground. If the lander isn't on flat ground, they might not be able to lift off from the moon.

You'd rather play it safe. You tell Flight, "They're missing the tracking landmarks by at least 3 miles (4.8 km). At this rate, they'll miss the landing zone."

Flight simply responds, "Understood." When no new data comes in from the LM, you get more concerned. Flight will be asking everyone for a "go" or "no go" for landing decision. Your data still say they will land long.

The other controllers say they are "go" for landing. Then Flight gets to you: "GUIDO?"

You hesitate. You have only a moment to make probably the most important decision of the day. Everyone in the room is staring at you. You are sweating. Finally, you take a deep breath and say, "Go, Flight." The other flight engineers heave a sigh of relief. But you still aren't sure that your decision was the right one.

Turn to page 54.

The crew continues its descent to the surface. The LM's computer had been calculating their altitude. Then the LM's landing radar kicks in. This system uses radio waves to get the altitude directly from the surface.

You hear Armstrong ask, "We got a lock on the landing radar?"

Aldrin replies, "Yeah, we got a good lock."

Aldrin prepares to tell the computer to accept the radar's more accurate data. He wants Mission Control to verify the data first. "Are you checking on the radar data?"

CAPCOM says, "It's looking good to us. Over."

Suddenly you hear Buzz Aldrin say, "Program alarm. It's a 1202."

You know what this means. The LM's computer is overloaded. It has too much data to deal with. It is warning you that it might become too busy to do its job of landing on the moon. The computer could give up working. If it does, you might have to tell the flight director that the landing shouldn't go ahead.

But maybe you just need more information to know for sure. You need to make a decision in about 20 seconds.

To call for an abort, turn to page 56.
To ask one of the engineers on your team for a second opinion, turn to page 68.

Any alarm is a great concern because the previous Apollo missions didn't get this close to the moon. If Armstrong hits the abort button now, *Eagle* would fly back up to *Columbia*, and then the spacecraft would fly back home without landing on the moon. The sudden firing of the ascent engine is a dangerous maneuver. Like the landing, it has never been done before.

You quickly decide that such a maneuver is even more dangerous than landing with these program alarms. You go to your engineer after all to get more information.

Turn to page 68.

You are an astronaut training for a future Apollo mission. Right now, though, you are the only member of Mission Control who communicates to the astronauts. CAPCOM is always one of the astronauts. He knows best how to talk to them.

During the descent to the moon's surface, communication with the astronauts is spotty. Program alarms keep coming up, but everything else is working well. The Mission Control room becomes quiet. The mission controllers listen intently to the astronauts. They are down to an altitude of 3,000 feet.

Flight goes through a round of "go" or "no go" decisions. Everyone responds with a hearty "go" when Flight calls on them. You tell the astronauts, "You are go for landing."

Turn the page.

About a minute later, Armstrong takes over manual control of *Eagle*. The astronauts are past their intended landing zone, and he must not like what he sees. There isn't much the Mission Control team can do now. It's all in Armstrong's and Aldrin's hands. You listen to Armstrong say, "Looks like a good area here."

Then Aldrin says, "I got the shadow out there." They must be close!

Aldrin updates Armstrong on their progress: "250, down at 2 ½, 19 forward." This means that their altitude is just 250 feet (76.2 meters) and going down about 2.5 feet (0.8 m) per second. And they are traveling 19 feet (5.8 m) per second forward. They are still moving forward fairly quickly.

Then Aldrin says, "11 forward. Coming down nicely."

Then you hear Armstrong say "Gonna be right over that crater." Armstrong does not sound tense. In fact, he's amazingly calm. You notice you are clenching the armrests of your chair tightly. You try to remember to breathe.

You keep an eye on how much fuel they have left. Armstrong is still moving the LM forward, apparently still looking for a good spot. You need to remind them of their fuel situation, "60 seconds of fuel left." You wonder if you should give them more warnings about the fuel. Do they know how close they are? Should you give them a countdown?

To begin a countdown, turn to page 60.
To decide not to do a countdown, turn to page 61.

In exactly one minute, the flight director will have to abort the landing if they have not landed. You have never gotten this close to running out of fuel in simulations. Soon, you say, "30 seconds."

You decide that they need a countdown, just like for the launch, so that they are always aware of the remaining fuel. Just as you begin to say, "Twenty-five…" the astronaut supervisor next to you nudges you and snaps, "Be quiet and let them land."

He's right, of course. Armstrong and Aldrin are NASA's best pilots, and they know what they are doing. But you sure hope they get on the surface right away.

Go to page 61.

The astronauts may not need a countdown, but you hope they get to the surface quickly. You hear Aldrin say, "Drifting forward just a little bit."

After 10 seconds of tense silence, you finally hear what you've been waiting for. Aldrin says, "Contact light." A sensor on the bottom of the LM's landing footpads turned on a light to let Aldrin know that they have contacted the moon.

You are not quite sure what to do next. You think they have landed. After a few more seconds, you say, "We copy you down, *Eagle*."

Then you hear Armstrong reply, "Houston, Tranquility Base here. The *Eagle* has landed."

Mission Control erupts in cheers. You need to reply to Armstrong quickly, so he knows you've heard him, but the weight of the moment surprises you.

Turn the page.

You begin to stammer a little bit and then say, "Roger, Tranquility. We copy you on the ground. You got a bunch of guys about to turn blue. We're breathing again. Thanks a lot."

According to the mission plan, Armstrong and Aldrin should rest for four hours. However, they are eager to get out onto the surface and get going with the moonwalk.

Astronauts Charles Duke (left) and Jim Lovell (center) kept in contact with the Apollo 11 crew from Mission Control.

To recommend the rest period, go to page 63.
To allow them to begin the moonwalk, turn to page 64.

You decide to check with the flight surgeon. He is the doctor in charge of making sure the astronauts are healthy. He says, "They're tired but otherwise ok."

You still think they're too tired for the moonwalk. The landing was taxing. You want more time to check the ascent engines and the guidance computer so they are ready for liftoff.

You say, "The flight plan calls for four hours of much-needed rest."

Armstrong replies, "You can come up here and make us wait." You smile at that response.

The flight director then says they can go ahead with the moonwalk. In fact, Armstrong and Aldrin had planned all along to skip the rest period, knowing they would rather get on with the moonwalk.

Turn to page 64.

Eagle is in order. The astronauts are almost ready. It is Sunday evening in the United States, and millions of people will be watching TV. You tell the astronauts, "You guys are getting prime TV time here."

It takes the astronauts a couple of hours to get their bulky space suits on. Then they open the hatch. As Armstrong begins climbing out of the LM, he opens a stowage tray that has a TV camera on it. This camera shows the world his first steps on the moon.

In Mission Control, you now can see the black and white image on the big video monitor. "We're getting a picture on the TV."

You realize it's best not to talk too much. When Armstrong begins the moonwalk, you don't want to interrupt his historic first words on the moon. You want the scene to just happen.

Moments later, Armstrong is at the bottom of the ladder. "OK. I'm going to step off the LM now." Everyone in the room waits, breathlessly. Finally, he says, "That's one small step for a man; one giant leap for mankind."

Armstrong then begins to describe the moon's surface. "The surface is fine and powdery. I can kick it up loosely with my toe. It does adhere in fine layers, like powdered charcoal, to the sole and sides of my boots. I only go in a small fraction of an inch, maybe an eighth of an inch, but I can see the footprints of my boots and the treads in the fine, sandy particles."

You acknowledge that everyone can hear him. "Neil, this is Houston. We're copying."

Armstrong gets used to walking on the strange surface. "It's absolutely no trouble to walk around."

Turn the page.

Next, Armstrong is supposed to get a dirt sample. If anything is wrong with the spacecraft, the astronauts will have to leave the moon right away. They would have already gathered this "contingency sample" to bring back. But Armstrong seems to be taking pictures instead.

You report this. "He's getting the camera now. We haven't heard anything about the contingency sample. Suggest we stand by for a minute."

The flight director responds, "Ok, but he has to get the sample before taking any pictures. Remind him as soon as he gets the camera."

You then hear Armstrong say, "I'll step out and take some of my first pictures here."

You understand Armstrong's desire to take pictures and look around. But the sample is important, too.

To wait, go to page 67.
To remind Armstrong again, turn to page 70.

You wonder how exactly you are going to make Armstrong pick up the sample. You think it's better to wait for Armstrong to take pictures and then remind him before he moves on to something else. Flight asks you again, "Did he copy your reminder, CAPCOM?"

You know Flight is doing his job in making sure this important task gets done. You need to obey his orders. You will need a good way to tell this to Armstrong, though.

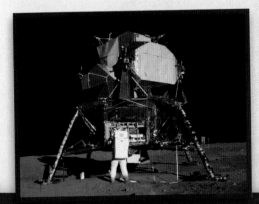

The gold-colored "foil" on the Lunar Module was actually one type of aluminum-covered plastic sheet. These sheets were layered on to insulate and protect the vehicle from space debris.

Turn to page 70.

"Stand by, Flight," you say. Suddenly the entire mission—and history—is in your lap! You check in with Jack Garman, one of the engineers working in a back room, "Jack, what do you think?"

You remember something similar happening during a simulation. Then it was a 1201 alarm. You had called for an abort during that simulation because you thought it meant the computer would stop working. It was a mistake. You should have continued with the landing. But now, you need to know if this is the same type of alarm.

Garman says, "It's a 1202. It's the if-it-doesn't-come-up-too-much rule." This is just what you need to hear. As long as this alarm doesn't come up too often, you can keep going. You quickly tell Flight, "We're Go on that alarm."

The landing continues. Then Flight asks for another round of "go" or "no go" decisions. The computer is handling the critical mission tasks. So when Flight says, "GUIDO," you say, "GO!" probably a little louder than you needed to.

The program alarms are slightly distracting to the astronauts, but the LM continues to perform normally. The landing continues!

Michael Collins photographed the Lunar Module as it returned from the surface of the moon.

THE END

To follow another path, turn to page 11.
To read the conclusion, turn to page 101.

You keep your reminder upbeat, "Neil, we're reading you loud and clear. We see you getting some pictures and the contingency sample." That should be a clear enough reminder but also does not directly contradict what he is doing.

Armstrong replies, "Roger. I'm going to get to that just as soon as I finish this picture series." The flight director seems resigned to this course of action: "Fair enough."

Next, it's Aldrin's turn to climb down from the LM and walk on the moon. He climbs down and stands at the foot of the ladder. "Beautiful view!" he says.

Armstrong replies, "Isn't that something! Magnificent sight out here."

"Magnificent desolation," adds Aldrin.

You try to imagine what it's like to be there. A stark landscape with few colors. Armstrong and Aldrin stand on ground that has never been stepped on before. You listen as they gather rock and dirt samples, take pictures, set up science experiments, and learn to walk on the moon.

After exploring the surface of the moon for about two hours, the two astronauts climb back into the LM. It's definitely time for a rest. They have been up for about 20 hours. And they have an important part of the mission to complete— the return to Earth. They'll sleep for a short time and then prepare for liftoff from the moon.

Another astronaut comes to take over as CAPCOM for the next shift. Feeling proud of your role in the mission, you begin looking forward to your turn to walk on the moon!

THE END

To follow another path, turn to page 11.
To read the conclusion, turn to page 101.

The USS *Hornet* crew and U.S. Navy swimmers were well trained in recovering the Apollo 11 astronauts from the ocean.

CHAPTER 4

RETURNING TO EARTH

You are on board the USS *Hornet* in the middle of the Pacific Ocean. A member of the U.S. Navy, you are part of the team that will retrieve the Apollo 11 astronauts from the ocean after they splash down. *Hornet* is an aircraft carrier with a crew of 3,448.

You and your crewmates are proud to be on this important mission. You know the world will be watching to see the conclusion to Kennedy's lofty goal: "… of landing a man on the moon and returning him safely to the Earth." This second part of Kennedy's goal is the heart of *Hornet*'s current mission.

Turn the page.

You have been on a recovery mission for Apollo before. But Apollo 11 is different. This is the first moon landing, and it has much more attention. More TV cameras, more reporters, more photographers.

There is another part of this recovery mission that wasn't part of the others. Since these astronauts were the first to walk on the moon, some people are concerned about them bringing back harmful pathogens that might exist on the moon. You think it's pretty unlikely that "moon germs" could spread on Earth and cause destruction. But you and the *Hornet* crew have to follow strict decontamination procedures.

Standing on *Hornet*'s flight deck, you look toward the moon and think, "Wow, those guys are up there now, but they're going to come back and land near us."

To work the recovery mission as an officer, go to page 75.
To be a recovery swimmer, turn to page 85.

You are one of the officers aboard the *Hornet*. The *Hornet* was on duty during the launch and first orbit around Earth in case anything went wrong and the astronauts had to return to Earth right away. *Hornet* also needed to be ready during the journey to the moon in case Apollo 11 had a problem and had to come back early. You have been a part of countless practice runs of the recovery of the capsule and quarantine procedures.

Soon before the expected splashdown of Apollo 11, you learn that President Richard Nixon will be coming aboard to greet the astronauts. You're excited to meet the president. But you know it also means a lot of extra pressure and preparation for you and the rest of the crew.

On top of that, a typhoon is developing in the planned splashdown zone.

To work on the presidential visit, turn to page 76.
To work on the storm situation, turn to page 79.

You meet with the ship's captain. The president plans to arrive on July 24, shortly before splashdown.

"This will certainly make us even more busy," says the captain with a grin. He assigns you the job of gathering all the necessary details of Nixon's visit so the crew can be ready.

It takes a few days to find out more details. Not only is the president coming, but also Secretary of State William Rogers, National Security Adviser Henry Kissinger, and Apollo 8 astronaut Frank Borman.

Besides that, reporters and photographers will be following the president. And of course, a large number of Secret Service members who protect the president will also be there. This group will be arriving in advance, on July 22.

The group's visit adds a lot more planning to the recovery mission. Should you have the crew do a practice run of the president's visit, just as you have done for the recovery itself? Or will that take up too much of the crew's time?

President Nixon (center) arrived on the USS *Hornet* about one hour before the recovery operation began.

To advise the captain to practice for the president's visit, turn to page 78.
To tell the captain that there isn't enough time for a practice run, turn to page 96.

You tell the captain that you think practice runs of the recovery should now include the president's visit. He thinks it's an excellent idea. "Yes, we should simulate everything about this mission so everyone knows exactly what to expect."

The advance party arrives on *Hornet* on July 22, one day ahead of the president. There will be time that day to work with Secret Service on where Nixon should stand when the astronauts come on board. You can get areas set up where reporters and TV cameras should be.

Go to page 79.

You meet with the captain and tell him, "A typhoon is developing in the planned splashdown zone."

The captain considers this. "Even if the storm isn't directly over the landing zone, rough seas from a storm that's close by would make recovery difficult and risky. We'll have to figure out where to move and coordinate with NASA."

The new splashdown point will be moved 215 miles (346 km) to the northeast. This is still a remote location in the Pacific, but will be safe from the storm. But this new location could change the recovery process. Should you recommend doing another practice recovery first? Or should you get to the new site as soon as possible?

To recommend another recovery simulation, turn to page 80.
To continue to the new site, turn to page 81.

You want to make sure the crew is really ready for the recovery mission. You recommend to the captain that another simulation be done first. You say, "The last-minute change of moving to a new location might distract them. They should do one more practice to make sure they are focused on that."

The captain considers this for only a moment. "No, it will take too long. We need to get this hunk of metal moving!"

Indeed, traveling at a speed of 21 knots, *Hornet* will need 10 hours to cover the 240 miles (386 km). You begin giving orders to move the ship, and communicating with NASA about the new splashdown site.

Go to page 81.

Hornet cruises toward the new landing zone. As it gets closer, helicopters go out ahead to be ready for the capsule. *Hornet* arrives before the capsule splashes down. Everything is going exactly as it did in the simulations.

You are placed in charge of explaining to President Nixon how the splashdown works and when the astronauts should be aboard. Nixon strides quickly over to you. He is flanked by a few Secret Service members. Nixon seems overjoyed that the mission was successful. As he shakes your hand firmly, he says, "Well done, young man!"

You stammer a little bit, "Yes, sir!" You have never met a president before!

Turn the page.

"They are just stepping out of the helicopter now, sir." You then explain to him that the astronauts are wearing Biological Isolation Garments, or BIG suits. These suits are made of a lightweight cloth. They completely cover the astronauts and include two air filters that they breathe through.

Once the astronauts were in quarantine, their BIG suits, decontamination equipment, and even the raft that had been used in the recovery were cleaned and sunk.

"The BIG suits are a precaution against any pathogens from the moon spreading here. It's not likely, but we have to follow this procedure."

The president says, "That's fascinating. Where are they going now?"

You reply, "Sir, they now need to go right into the Mobile Quarantine Facility. We call it the MQF. They will need to be quarantined for 21 days." The MQF is the small, sealed camper-like room the astronauts have to remain in during their quarantine.

Nixon seems to want to greet the astronauts now anyway. "Why not just a handshake from their president?" he asks.

To not let him greet them, turn to page 84.
To let Nixon greet them right away, turn to page 97.

The astronauts have to get inside the MQF right away and not come into contact with anyone. Someone even has to spray everything the astronauts touch with a strong disinfectant. This includes the ship's railing and even the deck they walk on, to kill any possible germs.

Besides, the astronauts were getting uncomfortable in those BIG suits in the warm Pacific air. They get cleaned up and changed into more comfortable flight suits. Doctors check them to make sure they are healthy. Nixon can now talk to them as they look out the window of the MQF.

Turn to page 98.

It is now early in the morning on July 24. You are one of the Navy swimmers who will help the astronauts out of the capsule and onto a helicopter, which will carry them to *Hornet*.

You are on the primary recovery team because you are one of the strongest swimmers and performed the best at the job during training exercises. With the whole world watching, no one is taking any chances on anything going wrong with the moon mission now that it's so close to being accomplished.

Added to the pressure is the extra job of decontaminating the capsule and the astronauts. In the unlikely event that any "moon germs" could get loose and cause destruction on Earth, strict procedures must be followed.

Turn the page.

Your superior officer told you that if any of these processes goes wrong, a 21-day quarantine would take effect. If that happens, he told you, "Don't even come back to the ship. You might as well start swimming for Australia." You know he is joking—at least you think he's joking. But the message is clear—even small details must be done correctly for the mission to succeed.

The Apollo 11 capsule is now floating in the water. You ride on the Sikorsky Sea King helicopter that takes you to it. You get ready to jump in the water to help get the astronauts out.

To be the first swimmer in the water, go to page 87.
To be the second swimmer in the water, turn to page 89.

The helicopter hovers just over the water. Wearing a wet suit, mask, flippers, and life vest, you jump from the helicopter and splash into the water near the capsule. The waves are high and it's hard to swim. But you're a great swimmer and love the challenge.

The astronauts were in communication with the *Hornet* while they parachuted down. But you want to look in on them to make sure that they are OK.

The ocean waves are about 4 to 5 feet (1.2 to 1.5 m) high. They rock the capsule. As you swim over to the capsule you realize it is floating upside down. You won't be able to look in a window or check on the astronauts. The first tasks will be to stabilize the capsule and turn it right side up.

Turn the page.

You attach a sea anchor to keep the capsule from continuing to drift in the water. This is not easy to do, as you bob up and down in the high waves. You grab onto a ring on the side of the capsule. You then attach a tether, which is connected to the anchor.

An extra huge wave sends the capsule quickly upward. You hang on tight, but the anchor is now attached. The capsule is now ready for a flotation collar that will stabilize it. Then the astronauts can come out.

Turn to page 90.

You see the first swimmer attach the sea anchor to keep the capsule from floating away. You and another swimmer jump in. You work to carry a 200-pound (91-kilogram) bag that has the flotation collar that will go around the capsule to stabilize it.

You attach the collar and it inflates. The capsule is now stable enough for the astronauts to climb out.

The flotation collar was designed to keep the capsule secure for the recovery operation, even in rough seas.

Turn to page 90.

The next job is to open the hatch and give the astronauts Biological Isolation Garments, or BIG suits. These suits are the key to the decontamination procedure. You climb onto the raft. The crew on the helicopter lowers the BIG suits to you. You put on your own BIG suit.

You drop the other BIGs inside the capsule. In a few minutes, the astronauts come out of the capsule. You first help Aldrin onto one of the rafts floating in the water. Collins comes out next, and Armstrong is the last one out.

When they are all on the raft, you need to close the capsule's hatch before starting the decontamination. But the hatch won't close. Its latch mechanism seems to be stuck. The astronauts have to be eager to get onboard *Hornet* and out of the BIGs. It's going to get hot and uncomfortable in the tropical Pacific air.

To just leave the hatch open and move on, go to page 91.
To keep trying to close the hatch, turn to page 92.

You have to get started with the process of decontamination and get the astronauts aboard the helicopter. You figure you can get back to the hatch later.

You begin to reach for the chemicals for cleaning the capsule. Then you see Michael Collins making his way back to the capsule. As the Command Module pilot, he knows all parts of the capsule, including the workings of the hatch. He works with it for a moment and then the hatch closes.

That done, it's time to work on the decontamination process.

Turn to page 94.

You keep working with the hatch, but with no luck. It's not like the one on the simulated capsule. Closing a hatch seems like a simple thing, but the mechanism is a bit more complicated than a car door. And it must be closed. Otherwise, water could get inside the capsule and ruin the valuable moon rock samples and film with photos of the surface of the moon inside.

The three astronauts watched from the raft as one of the Navy swimmers worked to lock down the capsule hatch.

Worse yet, if the capsule filled with water, it could sink. A sinking capsule would certainly make a terrible front-page photo in the newspapers. Even this was a crucial part of being able to call the Apollo 11 moon landing mission a success.

Michael Collins suddenly appears at the hatch. He moves the handle upward, locking it into position. He then closes the hatch. As the Command Module pilot, Collins knew all parts of the capsule, including the hatch. That problem solved, you move on to the rest of the decontamination process.

Turn to page 94.

You spray the top of the CM and all around the hatch with a soapy solution that kills germs. You spray the raft too. Next, you scrub the astronauts' BIG suits with a clear chemical spray that also kills germs.

The astronauts finally climb one at a time onto a net that lifts them onto the helicopter. The helicopter heads back to the *Hornet*.

With the astronauts on their way back to the *Hornet*, you take off your BIG suit and place it in the raft the astronauts were just in. You take the empty chemical bottles and the mitts used to scrub down the astronauts and place them in the raft. Then you deflate the raft and let it sink into the ocean. You are then lifted onto the other helicopter and race back to the *Hornet*.

On previous Apollo missions, astronauts were greeted with handshakes from the ship's crew. Not this time. The precautions to prevent "moon germs" from attacking Earth prevent such greetings.

The astronauts step off the helicopter. You spray a third chemical solution on the railings they touched. You also spray the deck they stepped on. Once the astronauts are inside the MQF, this part of the decontamination task is finally done.

You can now watch the president as he greets the astronauts.

Turn to page 98.

You don't think there's time to practice for the president's visit. It's more important to make sure the crew is ready to retrieve the astronauts.

You tell the captain about your idea. He snaps, "We simulate every aspect of this mission! The world will be watching and we can't let anything go wrong. The Soviets will be looking for anything to discredit our successful mission."

You say, "Sir, the Soviets can't be in any position to upstage us now."

The captain glares at you. "Our attitude must still be that they will look for any failure, however minor. You are confined to your quarters for the rest of the mission." This one bad decision means you will not take part in this historic event.

THE END

To follow another path, turn to page 11.
To read the conclusion, turn to page 101.

Reluctantly, you say, "Yes, Mr. President." But just then the captain steps in and says, "Sorry, Mr. President, but the astronauts have to get in the MQF first."

You were very close to breaking the decontamination procedures. If anyone had touched one of the astronauts, the aircraft carrier and everyone aboard it would immediately go under a 21-day quarantine. The ship would have to stay at sea until any possible "moon germs" were gone. With the president on board, that scenario was unacceptable.

Your superior officer sends you to your quarters for the rest of the president's stay. You are not able to help complete this historic mission because of one small bad decision.

THE END

To follow another path, turn to page 11.
To read the conclusion, turn to page 101.

TV cameras and photographers follow President Nixon to the MQF. The astronauts gather by the window. Nixon waves to them while everyone applauds.

Nixon steps to a microphone: "Neil, Buzz, and Mike ... I have the privilege of speaking for so many in welcoming you back to Earth ... as a result of what you've done the world's never been closer together before. And we just thank you for that. And I only hope that all of us in government, all of us in America, that as a result of what you've done, we can do our job a little better. We can reach for the stars, just as you have reached so far for the stars."

Armstrong replies, "We're just pleased to be back and very honored that you were so kind as to come out here and welcome us back."

Then, Nixon boards his helicopter. The astronauts stay in quarantine until August 10. They then go on a world tour. They talk to people all over the world about the mission.

You only had a small role in the mission. But it couldn't have succeeded without you and the thousands of other people who worked on it.

President Nixon congratulated the Apollo 11 astronauts on a job well done.

THE END

To follow another path, turn to page 11.
To read the conclusion, turn to page 101.

Mission Control kept a close watch
on every detail of the Apollo 11 moon
landing as it was happening.

CHAPTER 5

THEY DID THE IMPOSSIBLE

The Apollo 11 mission to the moon was a huge technological feat. Many crucial decisions had to be made throughout the mission. All involved performed exceptionally well. It had to be that way. It was such a big and difficult mission that every task had to be performed almost perfectly for it to be a successful mission.

The moon landing thrilled Americans, along with millions of people around the world. Parades were held in several cities in honor of Armstrong, Aldrin, and Collins. People cheered them as American heroes.

101

Landing humans on the moon was far outside what was thought to be possible. Kennedy's speech in 1961 had made everyone believe it was possible to do the impossible.

After Apollo 11, there were five more successful moon landings. The last one, Apollo 17, was in December 1972. No one has been back to the moon since.

The thrill of the first moon landing faded quickly in the 1970s. The government cut NASA's budget. There was no firm plan for future exploration of the moon. The country faced other problems, such as a war in Vietnam and an energy crisis.

People may not have returned to the moon, but space exploration continues. The space shuttle program developed and used the first spacecraft that could be launched and then landed on Earth like an airplane instead of splashing down in the ocean.

Each space suit and attached life support system used on the Apollo 11 mission weighed about 180 pounds (81.6 kilograms) on Earth, or 30 pounds (13.6 kg) on the moon's surface.

The International Space Station (ISS) is another huge and impressive space engineering feat. Beginning in 1998 the ISS was assembled in orbit. Space shuttles helped bring pieces of the station for assembly. After the station was completed, shuttles delivered equipment and other supplies to the ISS. The orbiting outpost has been continuously occupied by astronauts from several different countries since 2000.

Finally, the Orion program is testing new spacecraft that can carry astronauts to the moon and beyond. It took only a little over eight years to get from Kennedy's bold goal to actually landing men on the moon. Preparing to explore other parts of space might take longer. These missions may someday lead to astronauts landing on Mars!

The Command and Service Module (CSM)
in orbit, as seen from the Lunar Module.

TIMELINE

1957: Soviet Union launches Sputnik, the first artificial satellite

April 12, 1961: Yuri Gagarin becomes the first human in space

May 5, 1961: Alan Shepard becomes the first American in space

May 25, 1961: President John F. Kennedy challenges nation to reach the moon

December 1968: Apollo 8 orbits the moon

January 1969: Neil Armstrong, Edwin "Buzz" Aldrin, and Michael Collins are selected as crew for Apollo 11

July 16, 1969; 9:32 a.m. EDT: Apollo 11 launches

July 20, 1969; 4:18 p.m.: *Eagle* lands on the moon

July 20, 1969; 10:56 p.m.: Armstrong steps onto the surface of the moon

July 21, 1969; 1:11 a.m.: First moonwalk ends

July 21, 1969; 1:54 p.m.: Armstrong and Aldrin lift off from the moon

July 24, 1969; 12:51 p.m. EDT: Spacecraft splashes down in the ocean southwest of Honolulu, Hawaii

July 24, 1969; 3:00 p.m.: President Richard Nixon meets with the quarantined Apollo 11 astronauts onboard the USS *Hornet*

August 10, 1969: The astronauts' quarantine ends

OTHER PATHS TO EXPLORE

In this book, you've seen how events from the past look different from three points of view. Perspectives on history are as varied as the people who lived it. Seeing history from many points of view is an important part of understanding it. Here are ideas for other Apollo 11 points of view to explore:

+ The U.S. government spent a lot of money on the moon missions. Could that money have been better used to help the poor or cure diseases, or was space exploration just as important?
(Integration of Knowledge and Ideas)

+ Why do you think that the United States was able to beat the Soviet Union in the race to the moon?
(Integration of Knowledge and Ideas)

READ MORE

Bodden, Valerie. *Man Walks on the Moon: Days of Change.* Odysseys in History. Mankato, Minn.: Creative Education, 2015.

Green, Carl R. *Walking on the Moon: The Amazing Apollo 11 Mission.* American Space Missions—Astronauts, Exploration, and Discovery. Berkeley Heights, N.J.: Enslow Publishers, Inc., 2013.

Lassieur, Allison. *The Race to the Moon: an Interactive History Adventure.* You Choose. History. North Mankato, Minn.: Capstone Press, 2014.

INTERNET SITES

FactHound offers a safe, fun way to find Internet sites related to this book. All of the sites on FactHound have been researched by our staff.

Here's all you do:

Visit *www.facthound.com*

Type in this code: 9781491481035

GLOSSARY

abort (uh-BORT)—to stop something from happening

ascent (uh-SENT)—process of moving upward

commander (kuh-MAN-duhr)—a person who leads a group of people

contingency (kuhn-TIN-jen-see)—a backup plan

decontamination (dee-kuhn-TAM-i-nay-shuhn)—the process of cleaning something thoroughly to kill all germs

descent (di-SENT)—downward movement

module (MOJ-ool)—a separate section that can be linked to other parts

navigation (NAV-uh-gay-shuhn)—the science of plotting and following a course from one place to another

pathogen (PATH-oh-jen)—a microorganism that causes disease

procedure (pruh-SEE-jur)—a set way of doing something

quarantine (KWOR-uhn-teen)—to keep a person, animal, or plant away from others to stop a disease from spreading

simulation (sim-you-LAY-shuhn)—a trial run to practice a real event

splashdown (SPLASH-down)—the landing of spacecraft in the ocean

BIBLIOGRAPHY

Aldrin, Buzz. *Magnificent Desolation: The Long Journey Home from the Moon.* New York: Three Rivers Press, 2010.

Carmichael, Scott W. *Moon Men Return: USS Hornet and the Recovery of the Apollo 11 Astronauts.* Annapolis, Md.: Naval Institute Press, 2010.

Chaikin, Andrew. *A Man on the Moon: The Voyages of the Apollo Astronauts.* New York: Viking, 1994.

Fish, Bob. *Hornet Plus Three: The Story of the Apollo 11 Recovery.* Reno, Nev.: Creative Minds Press, 2009.

Hansen, James R. *First Man: The Life of Neil A. Armstrong.* New York: Simon & Schuster, 2005.

Kraft, Christopher C. *Flight: My Life in Mission Control.* New York, Dutton, 2001.

Kranz, Gene. *Failure Is Not an Option: Mission Control from Mercury to Apollo 13 and Beyond.* New York: Simon & Schuster, 2000.

Mitchell, Edgar. *Earthrise: My Adventures as an Apollo 14 Astronaut.* Chicago: Chicago Review Press, 2014.

Parry, Dan. *Moonshot: The Inside Story of Mankind's Greatest Adventure.* London: Ebury Press, 2009.

Shepard, Alan B. *Moon Shot: The Inside Story of America's Apollo Moon Landings.* New York: Open Road Integrated Media, 2011.

INDEX